WE REMEMBER

State Monuments and Historic Sites

by TAMERA BRYANT

We Remember: State Monuments and Historic Sites
by Tamera Bryant

Photography by p.1 ©Grant V. Faint/Getty Images; p.2 ©Joseph Sohm; ChromoSohm Inc./CORBIS; p.3 ©Bettmann/CORBIS; p.4 ©Bettmann/CORBIS; p.5 ©The Huntington Library, San Marino, California; p.7 top ©Buddy Mays/CORBIS; p.7 bottom ©Reuters NewMedia Inc./CORBIS; p.8 ©Bettmann/CORBIS; p.9 ©Illinois Historic Preservation Agency; p.10 ©Bettmann/CORBIS; p.11 ©Dave G. Houser/CORBIS; p.13 ©Lee Snider; Lee Snider/CORBIS; p.14 ©Buddy Mays/CORBIS; p.15 ©Galen Rowell/CORBIS; p.16 ©Bettmann/CORBIS; p.17 ©Oberlin College Archives, Oberlin, Ohio; p.18-19 ©Joseph Sohm; ChromoSohm Inc./CORBIS; p.21 ©Geoffrey Clements/CORBIS; p.22 ©Bettmann/CORBIS; p.23 ©Danny Lehman/CORBIS; p.24 ©Bettmann/CORBIS; p.25 ©Raymond Gehman/CORBIS; p.27 ©Photo by PDC Stephen Michaels, Wisconsin SUVCW; p.29 ©Dewitt Jones/CORBIS; p.30 ©Roadsideamerica.com Kirby, Smith & Wilkins; p.31 ©Roadsideamerica.com Kirby, Smith & Wilkins; p.32 ©Alain Le Garsmeur/CORBIS; p.33 ©Donna La Bonge; p.35 ©Bettmann/CORBIS; p.36 ©Bettmann/CORBIS; p.37 ©Nevada State Railroad Museum; p.38 top ©Hulton-Deutsch Collection/CORBIS; p.38 bottom ©CORBIS; p.39 ©PictureArkansas.com; p.41 ©Kelly-Mooney Photography/CORBIS

Nonfiction Reviewer
John Barell, Ed.D.
Educational Consultant, The American Museum of Natural History
New York City

Design, Production, and Art Buying by
Inkwell Publishing Solutions, Inc., New York City
Cover Design by
Inkwell Publishing Solutions, Inc., New York City

ISBN: 0-7367-1783-8
Copyright © Zaner-Bloser, Inc.

Web sites have been carefully researched for accuracy, content, and appropriateness. However, Web sites are subject to change. Internet usage should always be monitored.

Zaner-Bloser, Inc., P.O. Box 16764, Columbus, Ohio 43216-6764, 1-800-421-3018

Printed in China

04 05 06 07 (321) 5 4 3 2

TABLE OF CONTENTS

1
MONUMENTS HELP US REMEMBER

Lincoln Memorial, Washington, D.C.

History is not stuffy. It's not dry. It's life.

It's more than wars and dates and places. It's people and what they did. It's people and how they treat each other. It's the effect we have on each other—ten minutes, ten years, ten decades from now. It's our job to remember this part of history. We must understand it and learn from it.

Monuments help us remember what happened.

While a monument might be a statue or structure, it can also be other things. A monument can be part of nature, like a huge rock or a tree. It might be a beach or a field. Monuments can also be places where something important happened. A monument can be a home, a church, or a battlefield.

Devils Tower, our first national monument, is actually thought to be the core of a volcano. Many people visit this famous tower in Wyoming.

Devils Tower, Wyoming

Today the United States has hundreds of monuments in every state. They are in cities and towns across the country. You will visit some of them in this book.

These monuments help us remember who came before us. They tell us stories about what happened. Sometimes they make us cry. Other times they make us smile or even laugh.

2
WE REMEMBER PEOPLE

March from Selma, Alabama

A country is more than land and water. A country is also the people who live there. It's the people who work and fight and die there. It's the mothers and fathers, the brothers and sisters. It's those who stand together. It's those who stand apart. These people can teach us many things, but only if we pay attention to their messages.

The Chinese Memorial Shrine
Los Angeles, California

Many Chinese came to the United States in the late 1800s. They came to work and find gold.

The Chinese were one of the major forces in building the West. They were gold **miners,** farmers, and shopkeepers. Railroads, bridges, dams, and farms were built with the labor of the Chinese. They helped build the United States.

The Chinese Memorial Shrine was built in 1888. It is the oldest Chinese American structure in Los Angeles.

Chinese railroad workers

4

Chinese Memorial Shrine, Los Angeles, California

An altar stands between two kilns. A kiln is like an oven. Each kiln is 12 feet tall. The shrine was first used to honor the dead. When someone died, their belongings were burned in the kilns. Their families put food on the altar. They also burned incense. Today the shrine honors all Chinese Americans.

5

Crazy Horse Memorial
Black Hills, South Dakota

Crazy Horse was a great Native American leader. He was a Lakota chief. He spent his life trying to protect his people and their way of life.

Crazy Horse was raised like all Lakota children. He learned the Lakota ways. He learned to take care of others. He became known for his skills as a leader and warrior.

Crazy Horse fought to keep the Northern Great Plains safe for his people. He once said, "My lands are where my dead lie buried."

The Crazy Horse Memorial honors the spirit of Crazy Horse. It is still being built. A large model shows how it will look.

When finished, it will be the largest sculpture in the world. It will be 641 feet long and 563 feet high. The chief's arm will be as tall as a ten-story building. Mount Rushmore could fit into his head. A five-room house could fit into one nostril!

Can you imagine building something that large? Why do you think it takes so long to build such a memorial? Many factors play a part, such as weather, money, and mountain engineering. The builders go slowly because they want to get it right.

Crazy Horse Memorial and model, South Dakota

The Union Miners' Cemetery and Mother Jones Memorial
Mount Olive, Illinois

Mother Jones looked like a sweet old lady, but she was also a fighter for workers' rights. She fought for the children who worked in the **mills**. She fought for the men who worked in the coal mines. Wherever she saw **injustice** or unfairness she used to speak up and say, "There is going to be a racket and I am going to be in it!"

Mother Jones

The Mother Jones Memorial is in the Union Miners' Cemetery. It stands 22 feet high. In the center is a sculpture of Mother Jones. A coal miner stands on each side of her. Each miner holds a large hammer. The miners stand for the thousands that Mother Jones

8

Mother Jones Memorial, Mount Olive, Illinois

helped. She called them "her boys." Some of those miners are buried there. What does a sculpture like this teach us? It can remind us of the brave men and women who fought for the rights of others.

9

Ponce de Leon and the Fountain of Youth
St. Augustine, Florida

Do you know how the state of Florida got its name? Do you know who named it?

Ponce de Leon was from Spain. There, he heard about a special spring, or stream. Its water supposedly made people young. He called it the Fountain of Youth. He sailed in search of it. In 1513, he landed on the southern coast of North America. Flowers bloomed everywhere. De Leon was so impressed that he named the place Florida. This word means "flowery" in Spanish.

Ponce de Leon landing in Florida

Ponce de Leon statue, Flager College, St. Augustine, Florida

A statue of Ponce de Leon stands near the spring he found. You can see the stones that he used to mark the place. The stones form a cross, 15 down and 13 across. They stand for 1513, the year that de Leon landed on the coast of Florida.

The spring still flows. If you visit, you can drink from it. As it turns out, though, it won't keep you young.

11

FYI: For Your Information

Do you want to know more about the people in this chapter? Check out one of these books.

Colman, Penny. *Mother Jones and the March of the Mill Children.* Millbrook Press, 1994.

Cunningham, Chet. *Crazy Horse: War Chief of the Oglalas.* Lerner, 2000.

Gritter, Marissa. *The Chinese Americans.* Mason Crest, 2003.

Harmon, Dan. *Juan Ponce de Leon and the Search for the Fountain of Youth.* Chelsea House, 2000.

Kite, Lorien. *The Chinese: We Came to North America.* Crabtree Publishing, 2000.

Kotzwinkle, William (ed.). *The Return of Crazy Horse.* North Atlantic Books, 2001.

Kraft, Betsy Harvey. *Mother Jones: One Woman's Fight for Labor.* Clarion, 1995.

Lee, Kathleen. *Tracing Our Chinese Roots.* John Muir Publications, 1996.

Olson, Kay. *Chinese Immigrants, 1850–1900.* Blue Earth Books, 2001.

Wu, Dana Ying-Hui, and Jeffrey Dao-Sheng Tung. *The Chinese-American Experience.* Millbrook, 1993.

3
WE REMEMBER PLACES

Walden Pond Cabin, Concord, Massachusetts

Monuments are all around us. You can find them in many kinds of places. You can walk the paths and visit the home of a great writer and thinker. The cabin at Walden Pond commemorates Henry David Thoreau. You can look down into a **crater** that was formed 300,000 years ago. You can stand on the spot where runaway slaves hid.

These monuments are not markers or statues. They are woods, houses, and even holes. They are places you can touch. If you go there, you can feel history.

13

Diamond Head State Monument
Honolulu, Hawaii

Diamond Head, Honolulu, Hawaii

Diamond Head is really the crater of a volcano. It was formed 300,000 years ago. In the 1820s, British sailors found the crater. They thought it was a diamond mine. They were wrong. Still, it has been known as Diamond Head ever since.

Hawaiians call the crater Lea'hi. It means "the brow of a tuna." Look closely. Can you see the tuna?

In 1908, the U.S. Army built a trail at Diamond Head. You can take the trail up to the top of the crater. On the way up, you can explore the long, dark tunnels. A staircase takes you to the edge of the crater. The staircase goes around and around. It has 271 steps! From the top, you will have a spectacular view of Honolulu and the coast. This monument is also a National Natural Landmark.

Diamond Head, aerial view

Stop on the Underground Railroad
Oberlin, Ohio

Oberlin, Ohio, was an important stop on the Underground Railroad. Was it a real railroad? No, it was a name used to describe a way to help slaves get to Canada. There they would be free.

Many folks in Oberlin believed slavery was wrong. Working together, these people helped the slaves. They hid them in their homes and barns. They fed them and gave them clothes. They helped them get to their next stop. Runaway slaves who could make it to Oberlin were well on their way to freedom.

Painting of slaves being helped to freedom

Oberlin is home to many important sites. The Anti-Slavery Society met in a church. Many former slaves are buried in the town cemetery. A 6-foot monument stands in their honor.

Another sculpture is also there. It is a piece of railroad track. It honors the Underground Railroad. The track rises out of the ground and looks as if it will rise into the sky.

Underground Railroad sculpture, Oberlin, Ohio

Walden Pond
Concord, Massachusetts

In 1845, Henry David Thoreau moved to Walden Pond. Wanting a simple life, he built and lived in a small cabin. Most of his food he grew himself. He picked berries, and fished and swam in the pond. Studying the plants and animals around him was very important to him. He wrote about all of this in his journals.

Thoreau turned those writings into a book called *Walden*. Many people say the **conservation** movement started at Walden Pond. What did this

mean for the country? Conservationists take special care to protect forests, air, water, and all of nature. Those who read *Walden* may feel what Thoreau felt. He felt close to nature. He enjoyed quiet times listening to the natural sounds around him.

Walden Pond State Reservation includes the pond and the land around it. The land includes 2,280 acres of woods. They are called Walden Woods. Thoreau lived and worked here for two years. A small cabin just like his sits on the grounds. His statue stands nearby.

Walden Pond, Concord, Massachusetts

FYI: For Your Information

Find out more about the people and places in this chapter. Check out one of these books.

Bauer, Helen. *Hawaii: The Aloha State.* Island Book Shelf, 1982.

Burleigh, Robert. *A Man Named Thoreau.* Atheneum, 1985.

Guard, David. *Hale-Mano: A Legend of Hawaii.* Tricycle Press, 1993.

Haskins, Jim. *Get on Board: The Story of the Underground Railroad.* Scholastic, 1997.

Monjo, F.N. *The Drinking Gourd: A Story of the Underground Railroad.* Harper, 1993.

4
WE REMEMBER EVENTS

Civil War soldiers

We work and play. We move and make things happen. We try to make things better than they were. Sometimes the things we do change us. They can also change others. They can even change the course of history.

The monuments in this chapter remind us of important events that changed our history.

Pioneer Woman Statue
Ponca City, Oklahoma

Starting line of the
Oklahoma Land Rush

On April 22, 1889, thousands of people gathered on the borders of Oklahoma. They were on horseback, in wagons, and on foot. When the bugles sounded, they took off. They were racing to claim land in Oklahoma!

These pioneers quickly staked out their new land. Still, life was very hard. Some people went back home. Many stayed and started a new life. They built homes, planted crops, and raised families.

The Pioneer Woman Statue honors the women who came to Oklahoma. They faced the hardships and dangers of traveling to new lands. Can you imagine what it might have been like? They faced long hours of travel and work. They faced hunger, sickness, and sometimes battles, but they did not give up.

The Pioneer Woman is proud and strong. She holds the hand of her young son. She is leading him into the new land. This bronze statue is 17 feet tall. It weighs 12,000 pounds. Can you think of women today who lead the way to new lands, to new ideas, or to new ways of life?

Pioneer Woman statue, Ponca City, Oklahoma

Dahlonega Gold Museum
Dahlonega, Georgia

Have you heard of the California Gold Rush? Well, California was not the only state with gold! When gold was discovered in Georgia, people went a little crazy. They hurried to Georgia from all over. It was the nation's very first gold rush. The year was 1829.

Towns sprang up everywhere. The town Dahlonega was named in 1833. The name comes from a Cherokee word meaning "golden." The county courthouse was built in this town. The courthouse was a busy place. Miners brought their gold there. Inside was the office where gold was tested and weighed.

Georgia gold miner

24

Dahlonega Gold Museum, Dahlonega, Georgia

The first county courthouse was wooden. The "new" brick structure was built in 1836. Today it is the home of the Dahlonega Gold Museum. There you can see gold coins that were made in Dahlonega. Gold nuggets from local mines are also on display. Some weigh as much as five ounces.

People moved to many states in search of gold. What do you think happened as people moved to new places? Towns like Dahlonega popped up in many states. Gold was important to the growth of the country.

Civil War Monument
Milwaukee, Wisconsin

The Civil War was the saddest of times for the United States. We were no longer united. States fought against states. Brothers fought against brothers. More than half a million Americans died.

The North wanted to end slavery. The South wanted to keep it. The North wanted a strong Union. The South wanted the states to have more power. The two sides could not agree.

The Civil War Monument in Milwaukee, Wisconsin, a bronze statue, was built in 1898. It is one of many monuments that honor all those who fought to save the Union. The four Union soldiers of this statue almost seem alive. Three are moving forward. A fourth has fallen. His **comrades** carry on. One has picked up the flag. It seems as if they could step off the base of the monument and onto the street.

Have you seen other Civil War monuments where you live? Have you seen Civil War monuments at places you have visited? Describe the war monuments that you have seen. How do they make you feel?

Civil War Monument, Milwaukee, Wisconsin

FYI: For Your Information

Check out one of these books to find out more about the events in this chapter.

Alter, Judith. *Women of the Old West*. Franklin Watts, 1989.

Copeland, Peter. *A Soldier's Life in the Civil War*. Dover, 2001.

Masters, Nancy Robinson. *Georgia*. Children's Press, 1999.

Thomas, Joyce Carol. *I Have Heard of a Land*. HarperCollins, 1998.

5
WE REMEMBER ANIMALS

Dog herding sheep

Can a dog really be your best friend? Many people would say yes. Judging by the dog in this chapter, they might be right. Then again, a horse can be a good friend, too. Many animals have been known to be someone's best friend.

Animals of all types have always played important roles in history. Some have been workers. Others provided transportation or food. Some were good friends, **protectors,** or **rescuers**. This chapter takes a look at some of the animals who left their mark.

Old Shep
Fort Benton, Montana

In 1936, a sheepherder came to Fort Benton to see a doctor. His dog, Shep, came along. The herder was sick and died a few days later.

Shep watched as his master's body was put on a train going back East. Shep was left at the station. He was loyal to the sheepherder and waited for him. He greeted every train, thinking the herder would be onboard. Years went by. The station master fed Old Shep every day. Shep stayed at the station, waiting for his master to come back. Word got out about this faithful companion. People came to visit him. School children sent him gifts.

Old Shep, Fort Benton, Montana

When Shep died five and a half years later, the town wanted to honor him. The Great Northern Railroad put a painted wooden cutout of Shep next to his grave. A new cutout stands there now. It is made of steel. A museum displays his collar and bowl.

In 1994, the town put up a bronze statue of Shep. He is standing on a train track, forever faithful, still waiting for the sheepherder to come back.

Statue of Old Shep

Man o' War
Lexington, Kentucky

Man o' War is perhaps the most famous racehorse in history. He was a big horse who loved to win. People came from across the country to watch him run.

Man o' War's groomer died in October of 1946. Man o' War died less than a month later. Some say the horse died of a broken heart. His grave and a bronze statue of him are in Kentucky Horse Park.

Man o' War statue

Looff Carousel, East Providence, Rhode Island

Looff Carousel
East Providence, Rhode Island

Wooden horses are special, too. How would you like to ride one? How about going around and around on a piece of history? Hop on a carousel! In the early 1900s, everyone wanted a ride on one. They're still fun to ride now.

Charles Looff built this carousel in 1895. It has 62 figures and four chariots to ride. All were carved by hand. Glass jewels and mirrors decorate the ride. The organ still plays.

FYI: For Your Information

Find out more about famous animals. Check out one of these books.

Byars, Betsy, Betsy Duffey, and Laurie Myers. *My Dog, My Hero*. Henry Holt & Company, 2000.

Hyland, Hilary. *The Wreck of the Ethie*. Peachtree Publishers, 1999.

Mandel, Gerry, and William Rubel. *Animal Stories by Young Writers*. Tricycle Press, 2000.

McGinty, Alice B. *Guide Dogs: Seeing for People Who Can't*. PowerKids Press, 1999.

Price, Reynolds. *A Perfect Friend*. Atheneum Books for Young Readers, 2000.

Reeves, Diane Lindsey. *Career Ideas for Kids Who Like Animals & Nature*. Checkmark Books, 2000.

Singer, Marilyn. *A Dog's Gotta Do What a Dog's Gotta Do: Dogs at Work*. Henry Holt & Company, 2000.

Sutton, John G. *Animals Make You Feel Better*. Element Children's Books, Inc., 1998.

Vinocur, Terry, LCSW. *Dogs Helping Kids with Feelings*. PowerKids Press, 1999.

6
WE REMEMBER OTHER THINGS

We know that people make history. They might be alone. They might be working with other people.

Things can also be important. The things we find, build, invent, or create can change lives. Sometimes "things" make history. Monuments help us remember the roles that these things play.

From horse and buggy to the automobile

Nevada State Railroad Museum
Carson City, Nevada

Can you imagine what it was like before cars, trains, and airplanes? We can move from coast to coast in a few short hours.

Before 1869, the only way across country was a slow, difficult trip on foot or on a horse. What changed? The railroad changed everyone's lives. It crossed the nation. People were able to take a train to a new home. They could visit friends they hadn't seen for years. They could send goods from coast to coast. The railroad really did change our nation.

Transcontinental Railroad completion ceremony, Promontory Point, Utah, 1869

Inyo

If you want to see old trains, go to the Nevada State Railroad Museum. It has more than 60 train cars and **locomotives**. More than 40 of them were built before 1900. Most ran on the Virginia and Truckee Railroad.

The Inyo is shown here. It was built in 1875. It is the oldest steam engine still running in the United States. If you visit, you can ride Inyo.

Bauxite Boulder
Little Rock, Arkansas

The United States
entered World War II in
1941. All of a sudden,
we needed airplanes and
trucks. More and better
factories and machines
were needed. We also had
to have more **aluminum**.

World War II factories

Bauxite Boulder, Little Rock, Arkansas

Many of the things we needed to build were made from this element. The country started mining more aluminum. The people of the country worked as fast as they could.

One of the main sources of aluminum is **bauxite**. So, the country needed to mine more bauxite. Arkansas supplied nearly all of our nation's bauxite. To honor the people of Arkansas, a boulder was used as a monument. The Bauxite Boulder was placed next to the capitol in 1943. The boulder came from a mine in Arkansas. It weighs 20 tons.

Barnegat Lighthouse
Barnegat Light, New Jersey

Sailors have relied on lighthouses for hundreds of years. How do you think they helped sailors? Lighthouses warn about danger. They serve as guides. Their **beacons** help sailors find their way.

The waters around the tip of Long Beach Island are always dangerous. Swift currents can pull a ship off course. Ships may hit hidden sandbars.

Sailors along the New Jersey coast have a helping hand. They count on the light from Barnegat Lighthouse to guide them.

Sailors called the Barnegat Lighthouse "Old Barney." The first one was built in 1824. By 1855, it was in bad shape. A new structure was finished in 1859. It is more than 160 feet tall. That makes it the second tallest lighthouse in the United States. Although you can't see it from the outside, the lighthouse is really two towers in one. Inside the exterior tower is another tower.

Now the Barnegat Lighthouse is part of a state park. The park sits on the New Jersey Coastal Heritage Trail. Birdwatching is a popular activity in the park.

If you visit the Barnegat Lighthouse, make sure you climb to the top. You will enjoy the view!

Barnegat Lighthouse, Barnegat Light, New Jersey

41

GLOSSARY

aluminum (uh•**loo**•muh•nuhm) a silvery, lightweight metal that is a chemical element

bauxite (**bawk**•syt) one of the main materials in aluminum

beacon (**bee**•kuhn) a light or other signal used to guide or warn ships or aircraft

comrade (**kom**•rad) a friend or companion

conservation (kon•sur•**vay**•shuhn) the care and protection of natural resources and the environment

crater (**kray**•tuhr) a hollow area that is shaped like a bowl

injustice (in•**jus**•tis) an act that is not fair

locomotive (loh•kuh•**moh**•tiv) an engine on wheels designed to run on rails

mill (**mil**) a factory

miner (**my**•nuhr) a person whose work is digging out minerals or other matter in a mine

monument (**mon**•yuh•muhnt) a statue, building, structure, memorial, or historic site that honors a person, people, event, or thing

protector (pruh•**tek**•tuhr) one who guards, defends, or shields another against harm

rescuer (**res**•kyoo•uhr) one who saves another from danger or harm

42

INDEX

Words in **bold** type also appear in the Glossary.